HEALING CHURCH HURT

Walking The Path

Sheryse N. Henderson

Walking The Path Ministries, LLC
Northfield, OH
April 22, 2016

Note to reader: When referencing scripture it is taken from the King James Version of the Holy Bible, bolded emphasis of author.

ISBN-13: 978-1530010806
ISBN-10: 1530010802

DEDICATION

This book is dedicated to my husband. You are truly the love of God manifested for me. I'm privileged to be your wife. Thank you for praying me through.

Contents

Introduction

My decision to write this book was not easy. After much prayer and meditation I surrendered in obedience to the Spirit of God to share my experience. There are a few things I would like to explain before you continue. Please note this is not a "how to guide" on leaving a church. If your desire is to leave a church because of something that was said or done to you or around you, that you were not in agreement with; this is not the book for you. Please, sir/ma'am, go to your leaders and attempt to reconcile. I am a firm believer that repentance is for all and everyone should have a chance at restoration. I am in no way, shape or form in agreement with "church-hopping". I believe you should seek God for which assembly your gifts should be used. Petty disagreements, personality conflicts and personal opinions, about tastes and attitudes should never be the main reason to leave a church. I am in total agreement with what the Word of God says about the church. *"Not forsaking the **assembling** of ourselves **together**, as the manner of some is; but exhorting one another: and so much* *the more, as ye see the day approaching." (Hebrews 10:25)* We should be a part of a local assembly.

I am not advocating in any way the disrespect of pastoral authority. I believe pastors were sent by God to lead a congregation of people. I believe that those people belong to God and the pastor is their earthly guide to a closer relationship with God. As it is recorded in Jeremiah 3:15, *"... I will give you **pastors** according to mine heart, which shall feed you with knowledge and understanding"*. I have come to understand through my own experience that not all pastors have the desire to accomplish this assignment. Some have become dictators, controllers and manipulators of God's people. The Major Prophet Jeremiah goes on to say *"... **pastors** are become brutish, and have not sought the LORD: therefore they shall not prosper, and all their flocks shall be scattered"*. (Jeremiah 10:21)

The purpose of this book is not to discredit pastors that are fulfilling their assignments to the best of their ability. My goal is to enlighten anyone who has come under abusive leadership, that they may detect the unhealthy relationships and begin proper healing. This includes abusive leadership from pastors who've strayed away from seeking the

Lord and have begun seeking their own pleasures. This book is based on my personal experience; my perspective. Fictitious names have been given to conceal the identity of those involved. My desire is to bring light to this abusive authority that is running rapid in the church today. My prayer is that you will read this book in its entirety. Lay all presuppositions aside and allow the Holy Spirit to minister to your heart

Chapter 1
The Call and Assignment

I was raised in church by both of my parents, although never married; they instilled strong Christian values in my life. They both had very instrumental roles in their respective churches. My mom was a member of a very large Apostolic church in the inner city. She sang in the choir and served on the junior missionary board and women's council. She worked full time, went to school full time and went to church all the time. My dad was a member of a large Baptist church across the street from his childhood home. He was a choir director, deacon and trustee. He also worked full time and was in church all the time. There occupations were described as tedious work as well as their duties at church. This representation of church being work, formed my perspective that ministry should entail hard tedious work.

At two years old my gifting became apparent as I sang my first lead in the children's choir. Many stood in awe at the big voice coming out of this little girl. From that moment on I knew I was called to "work" in the church just as I had seen my parents demonstrate. Throughout my adolescent years, I sang lead in the children's choir, attended children's church services and Sunday school on a regular basis. At the age of twelve, after being baptized, I was allowed to lead devotion (praise and worship) from time to time at youth services. Throughout my teenage years my voice developed and would touch the hearts of all who heard it. I remember the mothers of the church would tell me that I had an "anointing". I had no idea what that meant, I used to think it was the power to make people cry in church. However, whatever this "anointing" was it came with a heavy cost. I was constantly tormented by the enemy to do the wrong things. I developed an attitude very early that I could live any kind of way outside the church as long as I did my work in the church. Now thinking back on it, that attitude was taught to me indirectly by those around me in my church. In my mind, as long as I would sing in church and do God's work He wasn't concerned with what I did outside the church. I later learned this is not the case.

The more my voice developed, the more resistance I would get to be able to use it. Jealousy had set in our local assembly and my leads and solos were limited. I come from a very large and outspoken family. Sometimes too out spoken. We were often frowned upon, which caused hurt in us all. There are leaders who are easily intimidated by people who have the call of God on their lives. No matter how rash these people can be, they need a shepherd that will cultivate their gifts and teach them in the way they should go. However, so many times because the pastor is insecure, they will excommunicate those who seem to challenge their authority. I was mistreated because of my affiliation, not because of any wrong doing.

The situation caused me to drift further away from church, God and any such affiliations. I would still attend regularly at my mother's command but I would come late, leave early and my mind was on other things the entire time I was there. I just couldn't understand how God would allow people to treat me this way, all in the name of church. Little did I know this saga would continue the next 15 years of my life.

After graduating high school, I had no clue of what I wanted to do but "church work" was definitely not an option. One night, I was at a friend's birthday party at a local bar. The first thing I noticed upon entering the party was almost all the people their looked very familiar. After a closer look, I noticed that all the people at this party were workers at my church, ushers, greeters, deacons, etc. Then I looked at the DJ booth and the DJ was our church's audio technician. I must admit this scene became extremely uncomfortable although I had the attitude that doing whatever you wanted outside church was ok, this had gone too far. It was then I realized the importance of being a witness of Christ in and out of the church building. As I sat at the table, I ordered a beer and began talking to some friends. A girl that I knew from my past began to give me dirty looks from across the room. My first reaction was to hit her in the head with the beer bottle, but right as I was thinking that God spoke to me. He began to tell me the consequences of my actions. If I hit her, I would be spending a great part of my life in prison, because she would die. At this point, His voice was so clear, I jumped up from the table, dropped the bottle and ran out the bar. My heart was racing, tears streaming down my face and my mind trying to figure out if that was really God or the effects of alcohol. Either way I vowed

NEVER to drink again. I got in my car and sped home.

I opened the door and the TV was on a Christian television station. As I approached the TV, the preacher said "You, yeah you". I looked around my living room in complete disbelief. He went on to say "You, the one who is coming in from the bar where you almost hit someone with a beer bottle". At this point I just fell to my knees. He said "God is calling you to Himself. He's calling you to ministry. He wants to use your voice to win many to Christ". I began to weep hysterically. I responded "yes" to God that night and decided to follow His will. This was a vow I would never take back. When I came to, it was morning and He began speaking to me from that day forth.

The next year was like a whirl wind. God began to move people in and out of my life. We were ex-communicated from the church my family had been attending for over 25 years. God placed tutors around me to explain the gifts of the spirit and to answer many questions that I had about the things He was telling me. He united my husband, Jon and me and spoke to us both simultaneously that our marriage was ordained by Him and we were called to ministry together. We both accepted this call. Jon is an anointed musician and worshiper. Our gifts complimented one another. A match made in heaven, in my humble opinion.

I wish I was able to tell you that everyone was happy for us; however, we experienced a tremendous amount of hurt from leaders in the Body of Christ. I remember one instance before we were married, God told my husband to leave the church he was attending at that time. My husband had been a member with his parents for practically all his life. When he went to meet with the pastor to tell him what God had said, the pastor told him it was not the will of God for him to leave and gave him the story of the young prophet out of First Kings chapter 13. In short the pastor told my husband that he would be destroyed if he left the church. My husband decided to heed the voice of God and leave anyway. Less than two years later that church disbursed.

I left the church I grew up in. My husband and I partnered with a small ministry for a short period of time before we were married. The leaders of this church tried everything in their power to convince us that we were not supposed to get married, even though God spoke to both of us and instructed us to marry. After we did not agree with their advice, they treated us the same way I was treated in my home church. They wouldn't allow me to sing, they would talk bad about us. God instructed us not to respond to their foolishness.

One day, we cried out to the Lord and asked Him to lead us to the place of our ministry assignment. After some time He led us to a small ministry full of young people. For the sake of this book we will call the church "Impact Church". The pastors, who we will call "Pastors Roy and Renee Lloyd" were a young couple who seemed to love God and God's people. Our first service, we were received with open arms; you could feel the love of God throughout the place. The building was not in the best shape but it was definitely a place we could help grow. The ministry had only been in existence a little over a year. It was in need of some "kingdom workers". We were so excited! We had finally found a place where our gifts were received and we could serve until the coming of Christ.

Pastor Roy was very charismatic with a prophetic gift. He would preach the Word with boldness and appeared to have a sincere heart for the lost. He seemed very passionate about witnessing to drug dealers and those living the street life as he testified often about living that type of life himself. His sermons were comical and uncut. Many praised him on his ability to "Keep It Real".

Chapter 2
The Honeymoon
(Years 1-4)

Our first few years at Impact Church resembled the honeymoon phase of a marriage. Everything was great; we loved God, each other and ministry. We had no children at the time so we were able to give most if not all our time to the church. Our duties in the beginning included governing board members, Ministers of Music, praise and worship leaders and pastoral support. I was specifically assigned as an armor bearer to Pastor Renee Lloyd who had just conceived a baby girl. We served our pastors well. Anytime they called for any reason we were there immediately upon their request.

The ministry was growing and we were in desperate need of our own church building. The board came together and prayed about the area God was sending us to minister. We were involved in the decisions of the location and purchase of the new church. We would finally have our own church, no more breaking down chairs and equipment and setting them back up for service. Impact Church would finally have a permanent place to call home. Through much prayer and many board meetings we were able to secure a church building on the east side of the city.

There was much work to be done to prepare the sanctuary for services. We worked nonstop around the clock to accomplish this great task. Some nights we did not even go home to ensure the church would be finished for its grand opening service. We were extremely over worked and tired; however, none of that matter because I understood at an early age "ministry" was suppose to be tedious and hard work. Once again, I later learned, this is not the case.

The Sanctuary was finally completed and we were able to have our first service. We were so happy. I think we sang and shouted for a few hours. This was ministry, working "hard" together as a team to accomplish a task to edify the Kingdom of God. We went out evangelizing in the neighborhood weeks before we officially opened. The souls were ready and we were prepared to minister to them.

The church's schedule was a bit extreme. We were holding some type of service, class or rehearsal almost 7 days a week. At Impact Church, ministry was a 24/7 job. Ministry often extended to our pastors' home. We were encouraged to separate from all relationships that were not with members of Impact Church, including family. Our new family consisted of our pastors and fellow leaders only. Let me be clear, this was not the mandate for all members of the church, just leaders who walked close to the pastors. We were willing to do whatever was asked as we believed God had assigned us to these pastors and had given them full authority over our lives. We had no complaints or qualms about the leadership requirements at Impact Church during this time because we all believed in the vision of the church and our man and woman of God.

Our pastors began to notice our dedication to the church and the anointing God had placed on our lives and began to elevate us very quickly. We were licensed as ministers within the first year of service and elevated to the Call of Elder-elect within the next year. During our second year Pastor Roy Lloyd prophetically proclaimed to the church that God said we were the successors of Impact Church and we were being trained to take his place one day. He also proclaimed by The Spirit of God that I was the Prophet of the house because of my prophetic gift.

After these two proclamations my duties changed drastically. I was removed from my armor bearer position with Pastor Renee and placed as the Chief Adjutant over all armor bearers and adjutants for Pastor Roy. I also became the full time administrator at Impact Church. However because of the lack of funds, these were non-paid positions. I began to preach and teach in Pastor Roy's stead when he was out of town. I had his style, charisma and the same anointing he demonstrated when I brought forth the Word of God. I had become the second in command.

We interacted wonderfully together in ministry and business. There was never a distinction between the two. Our relationship had become so close he had become my spiritual and at times seemed like my natural father. We went everywhere together and could talk about anything. We were both extremely ministry and business minded and our whole lives were given to the work of the ministry. He would speak something and I would make it happen. My ultimate job was to maintain order in the church and train up other servants just like me. I absolutely loved it. I lived for the following: The authority I was given, the accolades from him, the anointing I possessed, the approval I received, the respect I earned and even the overwhelming demand that was placed on my life. I worked 16-18 hours a day and did not receive any monetary rewards. The thought of pleasing God and my pastor was all the compensation I needed. This was it, I was finally living in purpose and answering my call. I was told these things on a daily basis and I loved hearing them. Just the fact of finally hearing a pastor say my gifts were accepted, respected and able to be fully used was a feeling I had never experienced before. Finally, I had experienced the love of a pastor. "Priceless!"

Chapter 3
The Tribulation Period
(Years 5-9)

There are a few things I would like to point out before we continue. When I arrived at Impact Church I was broken. I had been hurt by God's church and those who were called His leaders. After every trauma there needs to be a time of healing. When you are gifted and under unhealthy leadership, your personal needs may be overlooked by leaders. I revealed my story to Pastor Roy of all the hurt and pain we had been through. I allowed his desire for the vision of Impact Church to supersede my need for healing. I was still broken and unable to operate healthy in ministry. My suppressed hurt was a root cause of my performance driven obsession.

The honeymoon period lasted a few years. Let's be honest, after reading what that period consisted of, it was obvious there was a great deal of dysfunction. I did not recognize the signs of trouble that were there from the beginning. I wanted this to work. I began to notice the signs and convinced myself to "Charge it to their head and not their heart". I would constantly tell myself and others, we would NEVER leave Impact Church. I would scold others for mentioning the thought of leaving. Pastor Roy emphatically taught that serving at Impact Church was our destiny and if we were to leave we would be workers of iniquity. The Bible says God did not know the workers of iniquity and were cast into hell. Basically, translated in simple terms meant, if you left the church, you were leaving God. You wouldn't make it in to heaven.

My duties at Impact Church were very extensive without any compensation. This became a strain on my personal life. I would never deal with it because I was constantly made promises of increase by Pastor Roy. He would even come up with ways for us to create finances that would not take us away from ministry. One of these ways was becoming Foster Parents. Without going into details the effectiveness of caring for teenage foster children and working at the church 16 hours a day 6-7 days a week was an epic fail, needless to say causing a major strain on my marriage. During this trying time the pastors' marriage was experiencing some strain. It was noticeable, there were some marital issues between them. I conveniently overlooked it.

Pastor Roy's philosophy was God and ministry first, then marriage. We were often told that when it comes to ministry our marriage was second. Pastor Roy had more say in my house than my husband did. Time went on. The marital issues between Pastors Roy and Renee became more apparent. They had numerous arguments in front of leaders, inappropriate comments about each other to leaders and even frequent talks of divorce. Pastor Renee had completely stepped out of the day to day operations of ministry and her marriage. This, in return, added more duties to my already full task list in ministry and in their home.

Their marital issues became a major distraction to ministry. Pastor Roy could not focus. He was lacking in his preparation to bring forth the Word of God. He would fall asleep driving and his house was not kept to his standards. We decided that for the sake of the ministry something had to be done. I began to assign people to drive him to service, cook for him and his family on service days, clean his house once a week and look after his children when needed. Let me be clear, he did not request any of these things we offered. These services were offered for the sake of the vision of

Impact Church. I handled all of his personal affairs; banking, medical/dental appointments, paying bills, travel arrangements, etc. I was also the executive assistant for his personal business.

With the new adjustments in place, Pastor Roy was able to become focused again, actually too focused. He began to pour his life into ministry and business completely neglecting his family and requiring us to do the same. All the things we volunteered to do for him during his time of weakness became obligations and mandates. We went from helping our pastor during a tough time to being required to serve him in this capacity as the Man of God. If this was not bad enough, Pastor Renee began to express her disgust for me and there was constant contention between us. This once loving church, that loved God's people, had turned into a place of bondage, jealousy and fleshly desires.

In the midst of this very trying time, I became pregnant with my first son. I was completely overjoyed because my husband and I had been trying to conceive for 5 years. I thought the pastors would be joyful as well, but that was not the case. Even through my pregnancy, I kept the same rigorous schedule and all my duties. I was extremely tired and sick most of the time but I still performed. Although never spoken directly regarding my pregnancy, I could feel Pastor Roy's disgust. He even had other leaders tell me that the baby had taken my focus and I wasn't being "ministry minded". Pastor Roy began to make very mean comments from time to time. I was never allowed to be sick or miss any services or rehearsals. I was expected to perform. I continued to perform up until the day I gave birth.

After a week at home with my new baby, I returned back to ministry. The hurt I experienced through my pregnancy was surreal. I literally had given my life to this ministry. I was treated as if I had done something wrong by having a baby. One day Pastor Roy slipped and exposed his real issue. He began to say that because I had a baby it was hindering me from serving as I did before. He implied I was acting like all the other women. At that moment, I realized I was the only woman on his staff and he would often joke and tell others I was his "son". He nicknamed me "junior". I was taught to be very dominant and not show any emotions. I was lead to believe that emotions were signs of being a feminist and were of the devil. The baby caused me to be emotional, so my sole purpose was to get back to work, show no emotion and get back to who I was before, so pastor would be pleased.

Life had become extremely hard after having the baby; no matter how hard I tried I couldn't get back to the "old" me with whom Pastor Roy was elated. I would often miss things, forget things and would get easily overwhelmed. He would often yell and scream at me in disgust. Not only did I get reprimanded for my mistakes but I was also reprimanded for the mistakes of those under me and was encouraged to reprimand them in the same manner. Pastor Roy would say very terrible things about his wife and other leaders. I found out later he would say terrible things about me to his wife and other leaders as well. When I voiced my concerns about what was going on, he denied it and quickly begin to point out all the things I was doing wrong. So I strived to work harder and do better. I developed a fear of making mistakes. My phone would ring all times of the night with issues Pastor Roy felt needed to be handled right then. I found myself lying and covering for him and my own mistakes so I would not be reprimanded.

A year later I was almost back to the "old" me as Pastor Roy would say, when I found out I was pregnant again with my second son. I immediately fell into a depression. When I told Pastor Renee I was expecting, her response was "I'm sorry to hear that". She commented that she hoped I would fall down the stairs and miscarry. After Pastor Roy found out, he told me my son was a curse from God for not serving like I should have. I was completely devastated. He later recanted that statement but the damage was already done. I went through my entire pregnancy hating being pregnant. I still had the same work load as I did before along with caring for my one year old child. I cried every day during the entire pregnancy. I led praise and worship one night after which I had terrible contractions. Pastor Roy told me nothing was wrong and I needed to stop bringing attention to myself, so people would feel sorry for me. I went home that evening, my husband took me to the hospital and I was in full term labor.

During labor I received a call from Pastor Roy asking me if I had paid a particular bill. I just began to cry. There I was on the delivery table and he was asking me about "ministry". Once my son was born, I would not hold him because I was so angry that I had another hindrance to ministry. Shortly after he was born, Pastor Roy called my husband and requested him to come watch his children while he went out of town. I laid in the hospital three days by myself with my newborn while my husband was tending to the pastor's house. While I was hospitalized my husband decided I should get a tubal ligation because Pastor Roy said that if we had any more children we would be unable to do ministry. I was so broken and hurt, words could not express.

My son became extremely ill. He spent the first years of his life in and out of intensive care. This is when Pastor Roy recanted the statement that he was a curse. My son required constant care which took me away from ministry for a few months. The overwhelming sense of disgust radiated from Pastor Roy as if it was my fault my son was sick. Pastor Roy conveniently called my husband every day and had him doing something at the church instead of being home with his family. This caused a tremendous wedge between my husband and I. I began to resent both him and Pastor Roy. My son, was then and is still a blessing in our lives. He is a testament of a fighter and encourages us to fight with him. He brought joy in a dark place the minute he was born. Once my sons health improved, I jumped right back into ministry neglected my duties as a wife and poured myself completely into the church.

The demand of ministry became even greater after Pastor Roy decided to change spiritual coverings. We had to look a certain way, drive certain types of cars and live in certain type of neighborhoods. The church building had to be renovated to represent excellence. Our focus shifted from souls to prosperity and living the excellent life. We were required to give more money to meet those standards. All the new requirements were not necessarily bad in themselves. The excessiveness of these new mandates; coupled with the over worked staff and the apparent dysfunction of marriage, family and ministry had become the recipe for destruction.

Under the new spiritual covering there were some changes made for the good. Pastors Roy and Renee sought marital counseling. We were excited. Our expectation was the atmosphere of the ministry would begin to improve for the better. Through counseling, Pastor Roy was instructed to cancel some of the weekly events at the church to allow family time. Things were beginning to improve in their relationship but instead of sharing the counsel with the other marriages in the church that were also suffering, more of a demand was put on the leaders to take on some of the pastoral duties to allow the pastors more time to spend together. Basically their marriage was improving while the weight of ministry was shifted on the rest of us whose marriages were struggling as well.

As Pastor Roy's marriage improved his overall disgust for the state of the ministry became more apparent. What once was a blessing was no longer good enough. He always wanted better; a better house, better cars and even a better church. His focus was always on more or better. Eventually he decided we needed a better building. Now if you recall in Chapter 2, I briefly explained the process we went through to acquire our first building. When Pastor Roy decided we needed a better building, none of those steps were taken. He basically decided to take a more costly building in a more prestigious neighborhood without hearing the concerns of the board.

We went from a 200 seat edifice to a 1000 seat sanctuary. The new church was enormous as well as its operational budget. Due to the increase in the budget, there was more of a strain on the people to give more. There was also a strain to create finances to sustain the lifestyle Pastor Roy wanted to live. A ministry of excellence became his focus and he would stop at nothing to acquire it. He became a full-fledged "prosperity" preacher; straying from our original roots of holiness and godliness. He wanted excellence but he did not want to pay for it. He achieved it on the backs of his congregants. Impact Church was now in a larger sanctuary and still having early morning services at its original location in the inner city. We had to have an appearance of one church in multiple locations. The funny thing was, the same people traveled from location to location.

Pastor Roy began working on his temper and the screaming was not as often. Even after he was tempered he still walked in such arrogance and pride. His mere presence was very intimidating and we were afraid to say anything against what he said. Meetings had become a forum for him to tell us what we were going to do and for us to agree.

Anyone who challenged him in any way would be completely humiliated to the point they would never speak out again. The working relationship we once had diminished. He became the dictator and I became his subject. He continued to voice his disgust of who I was and wished I would get back to the "old" me. At times he could be very loving and friendly and everything would be great but at a moment's notice he would turn into this very mean person. It felt like I was in a verbally abusive marriage. I would cringe at his presence, never knowing what mood he was in. I was fearful all the time if he called, expecting the worse. Not once did I blame him. I always blamed myself. It was something that I was doing wrong. Here is an excerpt of my email journal during this time:

I am sending this email because right now I don't know what to do. I am so irritated and somewhat discouraged. But my main issue is I'm just downright exhausted. I'm so tired I can't even think straight. When I get into this mode I don't get anything accomplished. My head is pounding, my body hurts, and my mind is going constantly. I shared with Pastor two weeks ago about me being ineffective. I feel like I'm being pulled in 50 directions. I'm always taking care of others and in return doing nothing for me. Between School, Church, and Home at the end of the day I literally pass out. I love what I do in all three areas it's just finding a way to do it all at the same time and effectively. I know I need to train some people up and I am working diligently on that, but how do I survive in the mean time. I need some sleep but most of all I need rest. I don't like who I am right now I'm edgy, snappy and just unpleasant. I've never been like this before. Usually I can just shake anything. It seems like I am stuck. All through this email I'm using two words that I hate and that is "feel" and "seems". I've never been moved by feelings. They are empty emotions and a "seem" is bringing about something from two different instances and make them as one. I'm not void of the truth I am void of my mind being clear to meditate on it. Pastor keeps telling me that I am able to do everything that I am doing and because he is the man of God I continue day after day. But I seem to be going down a spiral as each day goes by. I'm not void of the blessings of God and the life he has blessed me with is phenomenal. I just want to enjoy it with minimal stress, a clear mind and rest. I spoke a word a couple of years ago about stop taking your rest and allow God to give it to you. I have been doing that but rest has not come and I feel like I'm about to run out. The scripture also says they that wait on the Lord shall renew their strength. Not wait as sit and do nothing but wait as serve. I've been serving and I need a renewal. I just need to be refreshed, rested, and rejuvenated to complete the assignment. Not giving up or quitting just a pit stop where my vehicle needs to be checked, oil changed, tires changed, and a drink of water. Then I'll be back racing.

If I could just get back to the "old" me everything would be fine. I worked as hard as I possibly could and for whatever reason, I could not get back to that place. I was often embarrassed by Pastor Roy in front of leaders. He and his wife would belittle my family and me behind closed doors but praise me in front of the people. He would announce that he was giving me lavish gifts such as cars, money and even paying for me to have a cosmetic procedure done in front of the congregation but I never received these things. He wanted the people to think he was doing right by me because it was obvious how hard I worked and how well I served him. He was all about appearance but never made good on his promises. Even through all of this, I still made excuses for him and covered him when people questioned his integrity. Others began to question his motives and had problems with his methods. I covered him and convinced them otherwise. I strongly believed not to expose the Man of God's nakedness. I covered him so no one saw his faults, even if that meant lying or being deceitful. He was never to be uncovered. No matter how hurt and broken I was, I thought this was the assignment God had given me and I planned to fulfill it until the coming of Christ.

Chapter 4
My Epiphany

Luke 15:10-32, is the story of the prodigal son. Some of us may be familiar with the story of how the younger son had requested his inheritance from his father. Once the father granted the sons request, he immediately took all of his belongings and left home. He wasted his inheritance on loose living. The point I want to use to begin this chapter is found in verses 17-18: *"And when he came to himself, he said, How many hired servants of my father's have bread enough and to spare, and I perish with hunger!"*

There may come a time in your life that you come to self-awareness. It is often called an epiphany. Webster defines epiphany as a sudden, intuitive perception of or insight into the reality or essential meaning of something, usually initiated by some simple, homely, or commonplace occurrence or experience.

My epiphany came in the midst of a major event. It was the Elevation Service for Pastor Roy. We spent months making sure this event was done in excellence, as Pastor wanted. A lot of money was spent on vestments, supplies and special guest. We were expecting no less than 1000 people to experience this auspicious occasion. I was very troubled by the event because the manner in which Pastor Roy decided to be elevated did not agree with what I was taught. Without going into too much detail, let's just say he was going against the Order of Elevation that had been set by others who hold this prestigious office. When I fearfully questioned his decision, he told me he was setting his own order. Evidently I was not the only one who had qualms about Pastor Roy's elevation. The Prelate who was supposed to conduct the service and actually lay hands on Pastor Roy, cancelled a few weeks before the event. Regardless of not having the appropriate people in place to affirm this elevation, Pastor Roy decided to go forth with the service. This troubled me greatly. I could not sleep because of the heaviness I felt in my spirit.

The week surrounding the event was extremely stressful. We rigorously rehearsed, confirmed everyone was dressed appropriately, confirmed soloist and solidified details of the travel arrangements for Pastor Roy's spiritual coverings. I am sure I spent the entire week at the church making sure everything was right. There could be no mistakes or it would be a dishonor to Pastor Roy. The day of the service finally arrived. I lined up the processional of pastors, handed out seating arrangements, provided those with speaking parts their programs and made sure Pastor Roy's vestments were flawless.

The service began; the processional, the saber team, the sacred elements, Pastor Roy's entrance and the opening hymn all went according to plan. As our special guest soloist was in the middle of her song, the power in the entire building went out. The sanctuary became pitch black. The entire crowd was silent. I ran hysterically to find candles and open windows to shine light into the sanctuary so people could exit safely. The officials laid hands on Pastor Roy by candle light. We received an offering in the dark, then the service was dismissed. None of Pastor Roy's ordination papers were signed by any of the officials. Outside, trees had fallen on some of the cars. This was no simple act of nature; this was an act of God.

At this moment, my "epiphany", the way we were operating in ministry and the things we were being taught, were not pleasing to God. Darkness has no more power than that which is allowed. God allowed the power to go out. He may not have been in agreement with what was going on. I realized I put Pastor Roy before God. I was disobeying God by doing things I was instructed to do by Pastor Roy that I knew was wrong. I began to cry out to God in repentance. I was trying to get back to the "old" me and God was trying to transform me into who He called me to be, not who Pastor Roy wanted me to be. I did not know exactly what it was but something was definitely wrong with Impact Church and Pastor Roy and Renee Lloyd. That night I prayed this simple prayer: "Give me the answer, show me the truth. Expose the enemy's devices. Let every lie be brought to the light, not through a familiar voice, but untainted territory, not any bias. Show me the right as well as the wrong. I need to hear you like never before. Reveal to me O Lord what you are saying about this situation. Wash me and I shall be clean, whiter than snow. I'll forever serve you and seek your face."

Shortly after praying this prayer, God began to speak to me about this situation. The Bible tells us that if any man lacks wisdom let him ask of God. I encourage you to pray this prayer regarding any situation and I guarantee you that God will speak to you concerning the matter. It may not be for you to leave your church maybe reconciliation is what God wants for you. Whatever it is He will tell you clearly.

Chapter 5
The Exit

After praying the prayer for God to reveal to me exactly what was going on at Impact Church and what He wanted me to do, He spoke to me. Seeking God for direction, He told me that my assignment was finished. When He spoke these words chills instantly overtook my body and I was overwhelmed with fear. This was not what I was expecting to hear. I believed that all the pain and hurt I had gone through at Impact Church could be rectified and I would return to ministry as usual. Leaving the church was an impossible feat. What about the people? What about what I had taught them in regards to leaving the church? Where were we going after we left? What about my destiny? Impact Church was my life. I had disconnected from my natural family. I had absolutely no one outside of the people at the church. I was the successor; I had planned to be at Impact for the rest of my life. Leaving was never in my plans.

For the sake of being clear, how I felt at the moment was exactly that feeling. As believers the very thought of change could frighten us especially when we did not "see it coming". At times, we would much rather stay where we are, hurting, than deal with the discomfort of what it takes to change. However, God never intends for us to remain in situations that may be detrimental to the purpose and plan He has for our lives. The situation and Pastors Roy and Renee Lloyd were not necessarily "bad", they were just toxic to my growth in God. I refuse to believe that Pastor Roy intentionally meant to hurt me, but hurting people hurt people. Now back to the story.

I was in such a state of confusion and needed to talk to someone about what God told me. I hesitantly decided to confide in Pastor Roy. I went to him and told him what God said. He basically told me that God was finished doing the work in me, but I was not done. Even more confused after the conversation with Pastor Roy, I decided to accept what he said and remain at Impact Church.

After that meeting with Pastor Roy our relationship became obviously worse. He began to accuse me of trying to be the pastor of the church. The strangest thing about that was, I never wanted to be a pastor. He would reprimand me often about voicing my unwillingness to answer the call to succession. The people at Impact Church held me in high regards at Pastor Roy's instruction, but now when people would compliment me he would often tell them "She's not your pastor". I had never been accused of trying to be the pastor or trying to start my own church until now. This was probably the most hurtful thing in my 10+ years at Impact Church. I always held Pastor Roy to the highest esteem. I never discredited him. I always covered him. I was his number one supporter, constantly promoting the vision and encouraging others to do the same. Why was he accusing me of trying to take his church? Several months passed and I began to notice that Pastor Roy was trying to replace me with anyone who looked capable. He began to talk to me less and less and then eventually hardly at all. Every new person he tried to replace me with, faded quickly.

God spoke to me a second time. It was time for me to leave. This time I went to my husband and told him what God said. My husband was not in agreement and told Pastor Roy. I was part of a two hour meeting outside in the cold with my husband and Pastor Roy telling me that I was not hearing God. The already strained relationship between my husband and I worsened. I even voiced taking my children and leaving. I felt so betrayed. I was the "prophet" that could hear God on everyone else' behalf even Pastor Roy's but I could not hear God for myself. I was very angry, at Pastor Roy, my husband and God. All I knew was I needed out or was going to die. I became very withdrawn and silent most of the time. By this point, I wasn't allowed to sing or preach anymore. Pastor Roy began spending a great deal of time with my husband even to the point I felt he was purposely trying to split my marriage.

One day I cried out to God, "What is happening? Am I wrong? Is the devil trying to deceive me?" God spoke to me the third time and said, "I am sending you to a place you know not. Go!" I went back to my husband and told him again what God said. My husband was still not in agreement. The vow I made before God to my husband, I planned to keep. Nothing and nobody was going to separate what God had joined together. I just began to pray that God would open his eyes.

My husband really did not know all that was going on behind the scenes at Impact Church. Pastor Roy would tell me not to tell him certain things because he wouldn't be able to handle it. If he turned against the church his blood would be on my hands. Unbeknownst to me, Pastor Roy had been telling my husband terrible things about me behind my back. He even made a statement to my husband once that if I didn't line up and get back ministry minded, God would send him another wife seven times better. At this point I did not care what Pastor Roy said. I wanted my husband and I to be released from Impact Church. If that meant I had to sit there until my husband saw for himself, then that's what I was willing to do. I had no idea this would take two years.

After praying that my husband's eyes would be opened a funny thing happened, my eyes started to open more. It was like God completely removed the blinders. I started to notice the sermons Pastor Roy would preach had very little scripture and sometimes none at all. Most of the interpretations he would give for the scriptures he did use were incorrect. His sermons became very inappropriate; they became very sexual in nature. Without going into too many details let's just say if they were a movie they would be rated PG13 and Rated R. His comments to and about other people were also vulgar at times. Thinking back he was always explicit but during this time he became a bit over the top. It had gotten so bad I could not hear him preach. I would be in service but my mind would be somewhere else. One day my husband came home and said that he was unable to receive anything Pastor Roy was preaching because some of the things he was saying was not sound doctrine. I was very happy to hear that but shortly after he was spending more time than before with Pastor Roy.

Pastor Roy was very convincing; sometimes to the point of manipulation. He had a way of convincing people to do things they did not want to do. He also would twist words and convince people they said something, which in actuality they never said. It was very possible to leave a meeting with Pastor Roy more confused than you were before you went in. His communication skills may not have been the best, but no one dared to tell him that at the risk of being humiliated. Many things were missed at Impact Church simply due to lack of communication. He often insisted he had given instructions that he never gave or that he said something he never said. Our communication was nonexistence by this time. I would communicate through text message or email so I could have proof of what was said. Pastor Roy became so prideful and acted as if he were God himself. He constantly complained about people not honoring him like they should. This was simply insane. He had more servants and security than President Barak Obama.

During Christmas, time before we finally exited Impact Church, my natural father decided to take us on vacation. My husband and I had never been on vacation since joining Impact Church. We had been on trips with Pastor Roy and his family but believe me, the trips were no vacation. My husband had accepted my father's offer to go with him on our first family vacation without Pastor Roy. Pastor Roy was furious. He spent the weeks leading up to the vacation trying to discourage my husband from going. He told my husband my family was just trying to get him away so they could convince him to leave the church. Pastor Roy also told my husband I was just trying to start my own church and if my husband allowed me he would have to answer to God.

The week before we were to leave for Florida, Pastor Roy began to reprimand me from the pulpit during his sermon. One time he ranted for about 2 hours. After the sermon, I went to him and asked him what had I done and he had said he would meet with us after we got back from vacation. While on vacation, my husband began to tell me all the things Pastor Roy had said to discourage him from going on the trip. The truth of the matter, Pastor Roy was upset because we made a decision knowing he did not agree and there was nothing he could do about it. He had major control over us and all his leaders and this was one time he lost the control.

After we returned from vacation, I was told I had been replaced by another pastor. We met with Pastors Roy and Renee and they told me many people had come to them telling them I was discrediting Pastor Roy behind his back and I was trying to start my own church. Even though this was not true I just asked that they release us from Impact Church. Pastor Roy told me to leave but he would not release us. We went back and forth for a while and I could tell my husband was still not in agreement with us leaving. Had I made the decision to leave, I would be walking out alone. I was not going to lose my marriage over this so once again I decided to stay. Immediately after the meeting, we met corporately as a congregation and Pastor Roy announced the changes in leadership. The new pastor had become the assistant pastor. Many people questioned what happened and why. I politely refrained from any discussion about the changes in leadership. Honestly, I couldn't care less, I just wanted out.

One evening I was getting ready to eat dinner and the worst pain I ever felt radiated from my mouth. I fell instantly to the ground and began to scream. This pain lasted about 2 minutes but it felt like eternity. Originally what we thought to be a tooth ache was actually a nerve disease called trigeminal neuralgia or often called the suicide disease. The pain caused by the disease was so excruciating, some people actually killed themselves because of it. The pain was so bad I could not talk, eat or drink. I was extremely sick.

Due to the severity of the disease, I was unable to attend service or work in the ministry. Most of my time was spent in and out of the hospital. I attended from time to time and sat in the back. I was unable to drive or care for myself so my husband had to care for me. Pastor Roy had laid hands and prayed for me to be healed to no avail. He then told me the issue was with my faith or I had hidden sin in my life; although neither was true. honestly believed that God had allowed this becaus I was being disobedient to His instructions to leav Impact Church. It had been two years since the firs time He told me and I was still there. One day I wa at home and fell ill and had to be rushed to th emergency room. The doctors called my husband a work and told him he needed to get to the hospita When he arrived, he took one look at me and sai that God told him we needed to leave Impac Church. I was in so much pain I could not respond, just nodded in agreement.

We were finally in agreement that God told u to leave Impact Church. How were we going to d that, was the question. Due to past experience w knew meeting with Pastors Roy and Renee was nc working. They would just confuse us and talk us ou of being obedient to God. My husband decided t take all of the items that belonged to the church phones, laptops, keys etc and put them in the churc and just walk away. I know most people may nc agree with the way we left, however we felt we ha no other option. The proper way to leave a church i to have an exit meeting with the pastor. In norma circumstances, you should inform the pastor wh you are leaving. As you can see, this situation was far from normal. We were controlled for so long we just had to run. That night we officially left Impact Church.

Chapter 6
Separation and Ex-Communication

After our official departure from Impact Church, I truly thought leaving would be the hardest part. Much to my surprise the aftermath was so much worse. Even though I knew I had to leave the church, I still wanted to have healthy relationships with those who were still members. We were more than just church members we had become family. We had a number of god children whose parents were still members as well as close friends. Due to the fact that we were always in church and never had time for our natural family, these relationships substituted as our natural family in many ways. We would eat together, spend holidays together and celebrate special occasions together. The very little leisure time we had we would spend together. These people had really become our family.

The day we left Impact Church I sent a corporate message to the people we were the closest to. It simply said God had ended our assignment at Impact Church but we still wanted to be apart of their lives and the lives of our god children. Each one replied privately. At the time they all agreed to keep contact, however as time went on we became more and more distant. We began to feel the tension between us and the members of the church.

A few days later I met with Pastor Roy to discuss our decision to leave. It was a very emotional meeting. I expressed the need to be obedient to the voice of God. The result of the meeting was Pastor Roy, although he did not agree, was releasing us from Impact Church. I was very pleased with the outcome because it was my heart's desire to be released and not just abandon the church. However, rumors began to spread that Pastor Roy was discrediting us to others.

The separation became overwhelming for me. It was as if my world had been turned upside down. I went from having friends to being completely alone. I cried everyday for months. I could not understand why these relationships could not be maintained. I loved the people at Impact Church and complete separation was the last thing I wanted.

One day I received a phone call from a member of the church. This individual basically told me that Pastors Roy and Renee called a leadership meeting to inform the leaders that they were forbidden to have any communication with us. The leaders were told that we were out of the will of God and that I was starting my own church and would try to convince them to join me. I was completely appalled. This would explain the distance and the tension between my closest friends and me. I never had a desire to start my own church. After it had been spoken so many times, I entertained the thought but dismissed it after seeking God's will for my life. Anyone who knew me, knew I would not encourage people to leave their church homes. I was also told, my husband and I were often topic of conversation and even talked about negatively over the pulpit during Sunday morning services. I could not believe after all I had done for Impact Church and serving Pastor Roy wholeheartedly this is the treatment I received.

I have been told by a number of people, when they decided to leave their church the other members were forbidden to talk to them. Some pastors incorrectly reference Romans 16:17, suggesting this is walking contrary to biblical doctrine. When did leaving a church, after being directed by God, become walking contrary? Not everyone leaves a church being directed by God or with good intentions. Forbidding people to communicate with them is a tactic of insecurity. If a member is looking for a reason to leave they will find one. Ex-communication because a member chooses to leave, is unnecessary if one is truly trusting God to add to the church. For those with misunderstandings, another member may be able to say the right things to get them to return. When someone desires to leave a church, no one should try to keep them against their will. A pastor's agreement is not necessary for their departure. The congregation should pray they find the will of God for their lives. The members should not tear them down and discredit their character.

As believers, it is imperative that we do not retaliate while separating from a church. Regardless of what's being said, let God do the justifying. There were a lot of things I could have said in anger to expose Pastors Roy and Renee. Let God deal with them whom He has called. He can deal with them much better than we can.

Chapter 7
The Angry Phase

At this point I was hurting spiritually and physically. The pain from the nerve disease was extreme. The pain of my heart was excruciating. I became very angry. Everything about my life had changed; my address, state of mind, condition of heart, church, health, friends, car, financial status and even my unwavering faith. I was angry with Pastors Roy and Renee Lloyd, the members of Impact Church and even God.

It is very important in this phase that no matter how you feel DO NOT forsake the assembly of the saints. It can be so easy to stop going to church. Once you get out of the habit it is difficult to go back. This is the most vital part of surviving church hurt. Isolation is of the devil. You will get even angrier being alone. Even if your heart is not right, position yourself in place to receive some type of care. I don't care where you go but find a bible believing church somewhere; no matter what denomination, consider it an Emergency Room. They may not be the best qualified or where you will end up but at least they can stop the bleeding or treat the trauma until you can get to a specialist.

My husband told me that God had given him instructions for us to attend another church. For the sake of this book we will call this church World Outreach. I had no desire to go to another church but in obedience to my husband I agreed. I had emphatically told God that I would never do ministry again. I would go to church, sit in the back and leave. I wanted no part of leadership, did not want a relationship with anyone and had no trust in pastors. I was very angry and I would keep my gifts to myself until I died.

The first Sunday we visited World Outreach I already made up my mind that I was not going to like it. I remember pulling into the parking lot of the church and immediately telling my husband I did not feel comfortable. When we walked through the church doors, no one greeted us. The greeter was on his cell phone. People looked at us very strangely and no one spoke. At this point I knew this was definitely not the place for us. We navigated our way around the church to find the children's church area for our sons, then preceded to the main sanctuary. All the people were standing with hands uplifted in worship. The music was definitely not what we were accustomed to singing. World Outreach was a multicultural church. We were not use to worshiping with different races. There was no usher to lead us to our seats; we had to find our own. After being seated I told my husband, once again, I was not comfortable and got even angrier. Why did God do this to me? Why were we here? Why couldn't we just reconcile with Pastor Roy? These people didn't even like us! Why was my life changing like this? I was not the one wrong. Why was I being punished?

At that moment in the service a white haired gentlemen began to address the congregation. He said that there was someone in the sanctuary that was in excruciating pain both physical and emotional and he wanted to pray for that person. My husband looked straight at me. At first I was hesitant because I was so angry but my husband urged me to go up for prayer. The man laid his hands on my head and instantly the pain stopped. I later found out, he was the pastor. The pain did not stop permanently. It stopped for a couple weeks which was a great sigh of relief.

Immediately after service we were invited to meet with the pastor in the church's hospitality suite. I knew God was up to something. What were the odds of having a personal meeting with the pastor the first day you visit a church. After speaking with him briefly, although I never spoke it, I could tell he saw my pain. His final statement to me that day was that World Outreach Church was a place of healing and welcome home. That statement touched my heart and even though I was angry that's the moment my healing began.

I received a phone call on Valentine's Day from my sister-in-law stating that I was on the front page of the local paper. She immediately emailed me the article. Pastor Roy had been indicted for public office fraud for over one million dollars. As his assistant, I was indicted as well along with his wife and four other colleagues. It all started a few years earlier when Pastor Roy opened a charter school for the benefit of the children in our community. This school was to better service our church as most of our congregants lived in a failing school district and therefore their children were not being educated properly. My husband and I were completely on board with helping the children so we signed on as board of directors as we were already signers on the articles of Impact Church. Pastor Roy also had an economic development company which was to be used to renovate and provide housing for low-income families that we were on the board of directors for as well. Pastor Roy would become the superintendent of the school and I would be the office manager while Pastor Renee and my husband were appointed to the school board. The school received an approval to open. Foundation payments from the state were not due to come for a few months. Pastor Roy did not follow state law protocol in anticipation of receiving these funds.

My pastor was heading toward a downward spiral of greed and I didn't quite know how to stop him. Numerous times I attempted to question some of the things taking place and was often scolded and instructed to do as I was told. I was extremely troubled. He became less concerned about the church and overtaken by business ventures and making money. The summer of the schools third fiscal year, I attended a treasurer's training class for charter schools in the lower region of our state. It was during this training that the troubling in my spirit was justified. I learned that many details regarding the business aspects of the school were illegal. My husband and I drove straight to Pastor's house from the training class to tell him all I had learned. I shared my concerns with him. He called the treasurer of the school. I am not sure of their conversation. He rebuked me saying I was operating in fear. He indicated, I went to one class and now I thought I knew everything. I was crushed. I worked the remainder of that year. I quit my job at the school. I couldn't take it any longer.

Unfortunately the damage was already done. Although I quit my job at the school and had left the church, a few years later I was still implicated in his fraud case. I was arrested, arraigned and publicly shamed all in the name of obeying my pastor. Not to mention the tens of thousands of dollars for legal fees. I was a signer on all three entities (school, church and economic development company). I was found to have had an attempted unlawful interest in a public contract to which I plead guilty. I received a Felony for this offense. (Felonies are received in various classifications ranging from 1-5 with the lowest, Felony 1, being the most severe. I received a Felony 5 Nonviolent offense with 6 days Community Service and Probation. A Felony 5 is just above a Misdemeanor. Both the Community Service and Probation were suspended once my fines were paid. I will be able to have this offense expunged from my permanent record.)

I was more devastated than words can express. Just too many emotions to list. God how could this happen? I'm a minister of the gospel with a felony. How could a pastor lead his sheep the wrong way and not even take responsibility for it? Not only was I broken, I was damaged. Due to the shame, I did not want to go to public places. Why had this happened to me?

Chapter 8
The Healing

When wounded, we tend to look at the person who inflicted the latest offense as the one who caused the most hurt. This is not usually the root cause of the pain. In my situation, I thought Pastors Roy and Renee Lloyd were the ones who created my initial pain. I later found this not to be true. Yes, Pastors Roy and Renee had done some very hurtful things; however that was not the initiation of my hurt. Had I been whole, I would never have subjected myself to their ungodly, manipulative leadership. I was wounded long before I attended Impact Church. I had not established healthy boundaries. I did not guard my heart with all diligence. I was not obedient to God. The duration of the hurt I experienced at Impact Church was self-inflicted because I chose not to stop it. Hidden wounds caused me to seek an overabundance of approval.

I did not come to these conclusions on my own. After experiencing such hurt it is imperative to find someone that can assist in the process of healing. For me, it was the transformational pathways class at World Outreach Church. This class may not be available to you but you must find something, maybe even grief recovery. Get to the root so that it can be exposed and eventually uprooted. If not, you may continue to experience hurt in every situation you encounter.

Once my hurt had been identified, the first step in my healing process was to find the amount of responsibility I had in the situation. I located how much I was at fault. The more responsibility I took for my actions, the less power the situation had over me. I took a large part of the responsibility in my situation because although my hurt was not my fault, it was my responsibility. It is not wise to despise people for what you allow them to do to you. At the end of the day, we are all a mess without the love of Christ shown forth in every area of our lives. Yes pastors have a responsibility to love people and lead them closer to Christ. However, because of their own dysfunction; this is not always the case. Most people think you just need to forgive and get over it. How can you forgive if you don't know where the offense originated?

There was a young girl named Nicole. She was 5 years old and was head over hills in love with her dad. One hot summer day she found herself extremely bored. It was too hot to go out and play. There was absolutely nothing that caught her interest inside. She began to play with the screen door. She repeatedly opened and shut the screen door. Her dog Sable, was monitoring her every move as she was known to run out the door when no one was looking. Her father told her to stop playing with the screen door because Sable would eventually run out. Nicole did not heed his instructions. Her father warned her again and again until finally he told her she would get a spanking if Sable ran out. Nicole did not heed the warning and open the door one last time. As soon as she opened the door, Sable ran out and up the street. Her father quickly ran after the dog. He caught the dog, he came back and gave Nicole the spanking he had promised. That was the last time Nicole would see her father for a long period of time. Although their separation had nothing to do with this event, she grew up dealing with rejection and always sought approval from every father figure she came across.

The little girl was me. I am Sheryse Nicole. Through my process I found out I had to go to my natural father first. I had to express to him 27 years later the rejection that I had experienced when I was 5 years old. Although my natural father had come back and reconciled, the wounding of rejection had never been healed.

I heard him say that I was never rejected and he always accepted me. The situation had nothing to do with his acceptance of me. At that moment the wound began to heal. It's like a cut that you keep covered up for 27 years; because it was never exposed to the air it could never heal properly. I just kept it covered. It still hurt when touched. It was extremely infected. I did not want to deal with it.

The second step in my healing process was to expose the hurt. I let some air get to it. I found someone trustworthy enough to reveal what happened to me. It was a neutral party. I was very careful to pray and asked God to show me the right person to assist. God does not want us hurting. No matter how bad a leader may have hurt you, He always has someone ready and willing to assist you. This was a very hard thing for me. Once trust is lost in pastoral leadership it is a very hard thing to get back. We must learn not to put our trust in flesh. Trust God to lead you.

The third step in my healing process was to process my emotions. I had to remember emotions are neither right nor wrong. They need to be expressed properly. This was difficult. I had been taught, in error, emotions were of the devil. Throughout this process, my emotions were all over the place. Sometimes I expressed three or four different ranges of emotions in one two-hour session. It was a long process but I worked through my emotions.

The fourth step in my healing process was to allow God to minister to my heart about the situation. I learned, when I truly allowed, He revealed my wounds and their origination. As He spoke to me He led me to specific people. Let Him speak to your heart without interruption. This step has no time limit. It could take months or years. Maintain a posture of being open to the Holy Spirit.

The final step in my healing process was to forgive. Forgiveness starts with forgiving yourself. One of the hardest things in my process after I took responsibility for what happened; blamed myself for allowing it to happen. I had to forgive myself, my natural father and the pastor I had served previously. Finally, I had to forgiv Pastors Roy and Renee. It was during thi process, I realized hurting people hurt people They suffer from their own wounds. They choos not to treat others right.

A bad scenario is for broken pastors to tr and shepherd a broken people. An evidence c hurting pastors is the constant hurting of thos who serve them. If you show me a hurtin ministry, I can show you a wounded pastor. have come to realize the importance of inne healing. If pastors refuse to look inward an receive healing in their own souls, how can the effectively minister healing to those the shepherd? I truly love Pastors Roy and Rene and pray that they too will experience this inne peace which comes through inner healing. chose to forgive.

Just because the core wound is identified, exposed and healed does not mean it will go away. Rejection still tries to manifest in my heart from time to time. I have learned the following:

Dealing with the core wounding of rejection is a lifelong battle. Although I have experienced Christ's healing of the core wounding, the tenderness of the issue is relived on a daily basis. One has to constantly battle the difference between actual events or residue of the original wounding. Battling this constant reminder of rejection is a tedious task. The smallest event can initiate the greatest emotional upheaval. My prayer is that the Lord will continue to strengthen me in this fight. I am accepted in Him by Him.

Please understand these are the steps that helped me survive church hurt. Although your situation and experiences may be different, I believe they can assist you in your road to survival. I am not a medical doctor or a psychiatrist, but I am a survivor telling my story to those who need to survive.

Conclusion
Starting Over

There are many devastating consequences when spiritual leaders are not using Godly wisdom while directing their flock. One resulting impact is the ministers and congregants under their guidance can be emotionally damaged. You do not expect to be abused by a pastor; it is like being "blind-sided". If you find yourself in a less than desirable situation – once you have come to your epiphany, allow the Lord to help. He can lead you to a fresh start.

Starting over was not an easy task for me. As I had stated in previous chapters my entire life changed when I left Impact Church. Starting new friendships, developing the relationship with my new church and pastor, as well as mending the relationship with my husband and family seemed to be an impossible feat.

While I was healing spiritually, I was also healing physically. Due to the severity of the nerve disease, brain surgery was required. Imagine, processing healing both spiritually and physically. Both required lots of time. There were no quick fixes. I couldn't get out the bed after the surgery and go about my normal activities. It took months for the pain to ease up enough to where I could function. I had many sleepless nights, being uncomfortable. I experienced temporary vision loss. My balance was off. I could not judge distances properly. I would tire very easily even at the simple task of walking from one room to another.

Ironically, I experienced the same things spiritually. It took time for my vision to focus so I could see clearly the plan God had for my life. It was very uncomfortable being in a new place forming new relationships. It was hard to use judgment and discernment properly. After Sunday services I became easily tired of the thought of it all. However I learned very quickly to take my time.

Once you've gone through true healing do not go and jump back into "church as usual". Take your time. Busyness can be a sign that there is an underlying issue you are avoiding. Do not hit the ground running. You may find yourself repeating old habits and ultimately, ending up broken again. Ease back into ministry. For me I started on the worship team. I heal through worship. That is all I did for almost a year. I could have jumped right back into leadership, preaching and teaching but it would not have been healthy for me. My goal is to operate healthy and whole. Be careful not to allow people to use you. Use your gifts while allowing ministering to your soul. I took time to establish healthy boundaries for my family and me. I realized I did not have to save the world by myself. Jesus is the ultimate sacrifice for us all. I am only required to be obedient to His word.

During my physical healing, if I did too much my body had a way of letting me know. If I overextended myself a few days, by the fourth day my body would literally shut down. There were indications that something was wrong throughout the first two days but I ignored them. Similar to what happened to me at Impact Church, ignoring the obvious. I had to eventually listen to my natural body. I had to learn to listen to my spirit. Train yourself to listen for indicators that something is wrong. Just as a smoke alarm lets you know when it detects smoke, your spirit will let you know when something is not right. It may not always be other people or the church you attend. Many times I find it is something in me that is not right.

It is very important to acknowledge the smoke detectors because they warn you most of the time before the fire is visible. However, where there is smoke there will eventually be fire if not tended to immediately. It is the same thing in the spirit. The smoke detectors were constantly going off in my spirit at Impact Church but I chose to ignore them. The fire had done much damage because I did not acknowledge and tend to the warning.

Spiritually, I now have adopted the same thing I was taught as a kid when there is smoke. Stop, drop and roll. The moment my spiritual alarm goes off that something is not right, a potential danger; I stop everything I am doing. I drop to my knees in prayer, earnestly seeking God to reveal what it is. Lastly, after I hear God's instructions I roll with them or carry them out. These simple steps lessen the possibility of experiencing extended hurt. I can safely remove myself from any harm if necessary.

Starting over was the most difficult thing I ever had to do but it was the most rewarding. To be able to operate in ministry healthy and whole is the greatest feeling. I now have healthy boundaries; I understand it's ok to say no. No pressure to perform, just to flow effortlessly in the gifts God has given me. I am healed. I am still on the journey. Inner healing is a life long journey. You always find an area in your life that needs healing; however, to have the tools to process it is the greatest gift ever. I am not saying hurt will not come again, I am simply saying you can survive.

I learned that God allows hurt and brokenness so we can experience His healing. I have also come to understand the only way to heal from church hurt is in church. There must be a series of episodes to replace the bad episodes in your life. As God began to talk to me regarding this, I definitely did not want to hear it. I was fine attending church.

God impressed it upon my heart to become member of World Outreach Church. With much hesitation I was obedient. After some time I was invited to join the leadership of the church. This was frightening. I began to have flashbacks of all the terrible incidents I had at Impact Church. The abuse the embarrassment, the open rebuke became all too real. With the constant encouragement of my husband, my parents, natural family and church family each new episode of church love replaced an old episode of church hurt.

And the Saga continues…

Made in the USA
Monee, IL
17 September 2024

66032273R00046